Your Free Gift

I wanted to show my appreciation that you support my work so I've put together a free gift for you.

"Retirement Cheat Sheet"

Just visit the link below to download it now:

http://pozittron.wix.com/musthavepublishing#!gift/c17z6

I know you will love this gift.

Thanks!
Scott Thomas

Contents

Introduction

Being secure financially is the chief concern for a lot of people over 60. Many people at this age are still working and are also in the final stage of planning for their retirement. Others have already said goodbye to the workforce and are searching for new ways to make sure that their retirement funds last longer. But the main question in everyone's mind at this point is how much money really is adequate enough to find happiness after retirement.

It does not matter how you spent your working life. Retirement is all about achieving what you haven't accomplished before. Before, you had to take care of responsibilities of family and securing your incomes. Retirement is the time to have the fruit of all your efforts.

We should always keep in mind that investment in a retirement account is not a one-time decision. It is more of a process. At one point, you would make an investment decision in a certain way, as the time moves forward, balancing that account becomes more and more important. Risk comes in many forms for investors. There is a possibility of a decline in stock prices. There is risk of erosion of an asset's buying power due to inflation. There is the factor of political instability which affects the international markets and the list goes on and on.

This book endeavors to incorporate a financial acumen in you so that you can plan an efficient retirement budget. For this purpose, we shall look at different retirement lifestyles you can pursue and try to estimate how much money you will need for your different life choices.

Further, this book explains the impacts of taxes and inflation on your saving budget and discusses how social security and pension plans can be used hand in hand to maximize their benefits. It then culminates by offering a brief review of further books you can read to have a better idea of each of these concepts.

Retirement lifestyle

Everyone's dreams are different. Each of us wants to spend his life in a different way. Even the concepts of comfort and happiness are relative to each person. Therefore to generalize a theory for retirement budget planning would be as insignificant as calculating how much income is sufficient for living happily. Planning a successful budget for content retirement does not necessitate having millions of dollars. The important thing is to first decide what kind of things you want to do when you are retired. An efficient retirement plan requires you to start your retirement after having secured sufficient amount of money to start lifestyle you envisioned in retirement.

Think back on what you wanted to do from the beginning. Some people want to travel the world, some want to try activities like golf, fishing, eating at five-star restaurants and visiting spas. This would require a much bigger retirement budget. On the other hand, there are those who want to stay near home and enjoy the simpler things in life like cooking, exercising or maybe just have a calm, leisurely lifestyle. You need to create a balance between being realistic about your expected savings and your expectations for your retirement.

Lifestyle options

Variety of choices

First of all you should know that when you retire, you become solely liable for choosing your lifestyle. It is a time when you are free from your responsibilities. You can now decide how to spend your time pursuing your very personal dreams. You can now indulge your efforts in doing things that were your passion since the start, but you could not make time for it before.

For some people, the change is scary. After spending a whole lifetime full of hard work, it is not easy to get start a completely different phase of life. If you are having difficulty getting used to this new life, try choosing a purposeful and consistent activity which can provide you with something similar to the responsibility of a job, thereby helping you adapt to this change. You can also try learning new skills.

They usually take up a lot of daily practice. Or you can become more physically active (which is also necessary if you want to take care of your deteriorating health.

Many happy retirees take on responsibilities of societal welfare work which they had not planned for earlier. Here also, the choice is yours. You can choose to help out your own family with their problems or you can broaden your vision and help out your neighborhood or maybe even the society at large. There is no limit to the possibilities.

Purposeful targets

There are two things a contented person needs; a goal and faith to achieve it. This theory goes on throughout life; when you are at a studying age you have the goal to get good grades, or for some to do well in relationships, when you enter the corporate world, you have the goal to perform well at work, thereby boosting your career, similarly when you retire, you need something to target your efforts on.

A sense of purpose is perhaps the most important thing in a retiree's life. All your life you have been working full time to provide for your and others expenses, now that you have been told thank you for your services and left without any such obligations, you are bound to feel a little bit useless. Hence, you need a good enough driving factor to keep you going through life.

Try to replace the same sense of purpose that kept you gratified during your working phase. Maybe now you don't think you should agree with this statement but later on if you have not found a purposeful activity, you will begin to miss this time terribly. Retirees who spend their times in just recreational activities with no other objective, soon find out that their life is not as contented as they had previously assumed it would be.

Reaching out

In many of the surveys, it had been observed that one of the most preferred modes of happy retirees is that they spend their time in doing constructive work for the community. You may find it satisfying to spend time in making the lives of others better. Since in retirement, you have much more time to indulge in activities that you could make time for both your recreational activities and in social work.

Like mentioned earlier, you can help socially by helping out your family or by doing good for the society. Each has its own importance. In our busy work lives, we tend to forget the importance of family and friends. There can be many who would need your help or just your words of encouragement to set their lives right. You can reach out to the relatives you have been shunning for years. Try to set things right. You can spend time with your grandchildren and help out your kids in raising a virtuous family while maintaining the work-life balance.

You can also start a life in the social sector. You have gotten so much from the society. It is your job to pay it back with your services. Think about how much time you want to spend in these activities. Research a bit on organizations close to you and find out which group's activity appeal most to you. The options are a lot; there can be service organizations, older people's organizations, environmental groups, Handicap welfares, school and church groups, etc. You can easily set up your priorities and figure out a welfare sector that matches it.

Conquering the world

Then there is this whole new side of retirement where the whole world is open to you. Nature has made each place a uniqueness of its own accord. There is beauty to be seen everywhere. Plus there are different cultures to explore and different people to meet.

Nearly every person wants to enjoy trips to other countries but could not do so due to their busy schedules. Some do manage to have this luxury but even for them, the possibilities, world offer, are limitless. The destinations depend on your finances; there are multiple enjoyable possibilities for whatever budget range you might have. You can find travel agencies that function according to your needs. Some of them provide specialized services for guided tours while some cater to the special needs of older people.

Retirement savings: A top financial priority

Here comes the dreaded topic we have been baffling you about since the beginning. By now you have probably started saving some amount from your wages, and if you haven't, don't worry as there is no such thing as being late in doing the right thing.

Either way, when you start thinking about the specifics of retirement lifestyle you want, you would want to make some rearrangement in your budget planning.

Depending on whether you want to enjoy humbler activities or a luscious living standard, you should increase or decrease your contribution level. If you have to increase your savings, you might think about taking fewer trips to restaurants, eliminating excess spending or maybe even taking up some freelancing if you are not making adequate money now. Just basically whatever you have to do to make enough money for the time when you will not have a healthy income source.

Paying yourself through a general savings account

Some of the money is automatically deducted from your paycheck in terms of 401(k) contribution. You can consider using the similar model for further saving up for retirement budget. Formulate a strategy to have automatic deductions to your savings account from each paycheck. It has been a general observation that people who have a healthy savings account are better suited to cope with financial emergencies. This way you can also avoid depleting your retirement savings account and well, emergencies do not come every day so in the end, you would most possibly have a good enough cash saved up.

Making this process automatic is necessary as it is imperative that you do not miss any payments. By making a habit of this, you can avoid this risk completely and also evade the temptations that always accompany whatever income is coming to you.

Doing the math

The last thing you want when you are retired s to be surprised to find out that there is no money in your savings account. Don't worry it is not likely to happen if you are a careful saver. What is more likely, however, is that you fall into the trap of generalizing your savings. It is important that you consider all the research which scholars did so that you have a comfortable retirement, but it is equally, or perhaps more important, to keep in mind that these only show the averages, which means that you should see those plans as the amount that general public uses but do amendments to suit your retirement needs.

Do an analysis of your account, see that you are saving enough money regularly which will add up to the adequate amount you require for your having your visualized retirement lifestyle. You would like to think about investment sources where you can put your money in for later returns, but along with that you would also need to have liquid money in hand which does not involve any risks.

If the equation does not seem to be adding up to a decent amount, then there can be two ways to make adjustments to it. One approach is to make more money. If you are at a stable job that is providing enough money to satisfy your needs, you need to pay equal importance to the need for saving up for retirement. You might want to switch jobs so that you can ensure a healthy paycheck every month. If that is not an option that can be pursued so easily, then you can think about having some side careers. Doing freelance work is an excellent option which does not bind you to a specific responsibility and you can do it whenever you can take out time from your work. Plus there is a very high demand of freelancers which warrants them a good enough income that is at the very least sufficient enough for your retirement savings.

Another option is to spend less. If you cannot spare enough time to think about other sources of income, then you can try to reduce your expenditure. There are always some costs that can be cut down. Average Americans spend a lot on eating out. If you can reduce just those costs, it can add up to a very high saving balance each month.

You can also think about eliminating memberships of clubs or other such places that you no longer visit. There will always be time to do such activities later on.

Like we said earlier, if the things are not working out for you, you can always make alterations to your retirement expectations. You can retire late and spend more time in making money, not to mention, the social security payments will also be increased if you retire late. We shall explain how in later chapters. You can also try to work part-time in retirement. Again freelance work is quite a viable option and then there is also the possibility of taking up teaching young people. There is unseen pleasure in transferring your knowledge and experience to others.

The best approach to this is to first decide upon your retirement lifestyle and then make adjustments according to the expenses associated with it. The best method of it is to have a budget breakdown. Catalogue your lifestyle expectations into smaller segments and estimate the costs for each segment. Then add them up and you will get a rough idea of how much you will need in retirement. Do not forget the factors of inflation and floating return rates. These will be explained in detail in later chapters. Right now you should know that these factors also play a critical role in determining the actual purchasing value of your savings. By taking care of these elements, you can have a comfortable retirement.

Money and retirement

Whether your career has been a successful one or somewhat modest, as you near its culmination, you should realize that you are looking at 20 or perhaps more years of retirement. The opportunities at this point are too many but somewhat frightening too. Obviously you do not want to waste your remaining time. So how would you work out all the different choices? How would you find out what will give you meaning in the upcoming phase of your life?

To answer this question, many scholars did a lot of research, mainly testing that whether money is the core source of a retiree's happiness or not. The answer they found out was quite complex. To begin with, the researchers found out that money can provide happiness only up to a certain limit. What creates the real difference is "how" we are going to spend our money.

They sought these answers from the people who have retired and seem to be living a content life and concluded that a happy retiree knows what exactly he has saved the money for. When he began planning for retirement, he had a specific purpose, a precise goal which functioned as a driving force behind his actions. Financial gurus concluded that this is perhaps the most critical point in planning for retirement, whether you start it early or late. Once you know for sure what exactly it is that you want to do or to be in retirement, only then your planning can begin to make sense.

For this, you need to get started with some hobbies. Think what you always wanted to do. Then take time out of your work to try it. You cannot be a 24/7 worker and then try to find out what to do with your life. It is not a healthy activity. You should have a core pursuit and it is very important to establish it as early as possible.

The adequate amount

Let's generalize our problem. Are the people who have more wealth happier than others? According to a recent research done by the economist Augus Deaton and psychologist Daniel Kahneman, money can certainly buy people happiness but only up to the limit of $75,000 per year and making more money will not make you happier.

There are those people who have not yet attained financial freedom. For them, there are a lot of options regardless of the age they are at. Most people over 60 worry that there is no or little chance for them to start a new investment, but that is not true at all. There are still many options. One apparent way to redefine retirement is to start a business.

Even if you are too uncertain about new investments, which you shouldn't be, by the way, you can also find ways to get more happiness out of every spent dollar. Mostly it has been observed contrary to the popular belief that buying things does not really make people happy as much as spending in themselves and their passions.

Predictable paychecks

There is no doubt about the fact that more money you amass, happier you are at least up to the limit of $75000 per year. Once you have built up a comfortable amount, the effect declines. Wes Moss surveyed 1,400 retirees in 46 states. He inferred from the survey that where your money comes from is as much important as the amount of savings you have. The retirees who have a predictable income source, for example, a pension or rental properties, get more happiness from spending that money than they do so by using income from a 401(k) or an IRA.

Likewise, a Towers Watson happiness survey found out that retirees with the greatest financial anxiety are the ones who rely majorly for income from investments. About a third of the retirees who get less than a quarter of their money from pensions or an annuity are concerned about their financial security, while among those who received more than half of their funds from a predictable income source more than 75% are quite content with their financial position.

A common practice among retirees is that they tend to switch careers in retirement to gain monetary security which is not as beneficial as people might think. Yujie Zhan, a researcher from Laurier University, says that "Retirees who take jobs in their field reported the best mental health perhaps because adapting to a new work environment and duties is stressful."

Experiences Vs Stuff

Researchers were quite surprised when they found out that contentment in retirement is not that much based on the amount of money you managed to save up but actually on how you can use it to pursue your most enjoyable activities. Maybe this is why the saying "money cannot buy happiness" became so famous because it holds true when it comes to a whole world of things.

Buying a new pair of shoes or a hand bad or a cool gadget does indeed gives a quick lift off to our emotions but it is only short term and the feeling dwindles quickly. However, same cannot be said for memorable experiences. They are there to stay. And they still have the power to bring smiles to our faces even after years had passed.

One should not forget the power of nostalgia. Remembering all those laughs you had with your friends when you were young still makes you smile with joy. This nostalgia keeps our brain healthy and happy. When you capitalize in experiences, you are building a reservoir of memories that you can u can return to use again and again and it can never run out.

Getting out into the world, pursue your hobbies and dreams, taking trips or organizing coffee dates with your best friends are the small pieces of the puzzle that can build a contented retirement. Investing time and money in forming social connections provides the key to having unforgettable experiences that will energize your life and enrich your pleasure. So to give the biggest boost to happiness, we need to pick hobbies that are social in nature. On observation, it has been found that the happiest of the retirees have hobbies like volunteering, travelling, golf while the unhappy lot pursued reading, hunting, fishing, and writing. Happy people tend to not do things in isolation.

We have also seen very frequently that busy retirees are always happier than those who have no work to do. But here also comes another question; just how much active do you need to be? The researcher we mentioned earlier, Moss, has given us a number for the answer. He found out from his studies that the happiest class of retirees was handling three to four activities regularly while the least happy had only one or two. Also, the happy retirees had an extremely busy schedule. He called it "Hobbies on steroids".

Getting Out of Debt

This is perhaps the most crucial element we have to take care of in our youth and the one most of us are likely to neglect. At the first opportunity you get, tackle your mortgage and if you do not have such an opportunity then create one. It can become the most critical obstacle in your later years, especially after retirement when the income sources are limited and you do not want the ghost of your past debts coming back to haunt you.

As the years to pay mortgage off go down, the happiness level rises. And disagreeing with popular belief, there are actually a lot of ways to do so. If you can pay your debt off with non-retirement money, pay it off in one go. Or if that is not possible, then you can pay off additional $100, $200, or $300 dollars a month. It can shear a whole ten years off a 30-year mortgage.

True we have established that having a huge amount of money in your bank account may not make you happier but if you have a huge debt, it would certainly take your happiness away. There are very few things that are more stressful than the thought of dealing with creditors. Also, every dollar spent in paying off debt cuts short every buck that you can't spend on activities that can naturally make you happy.

That is all when paying off debt is easy enough that you can do it anytime. For some of you, debt would have become unmanageable. Don't freak out at that, every problem has a simple solution. Seek advice from a financial advisor of good reputation or take help from any good debt support group. Try to heed their advice, make efforts to correct your mistake and not bury your head in the sand.

Paying off mortgage can easily become the difference between a happy retirement and a stressful one. Although the more you pay off, the less you would have for the time being but you can keep more to work with later on. In addition to that, it has been a common observation that paying off even a small amount each month removes stress incredibly and gives people a sense of being in control of their life. Also paying off the stress of debt frees your mind which allows it to search for different sources of income and let you chase your passions freely.

What affect does a successful adulthood has on retirement

Having said that, it has also been confirmed by research that people who had a doomed adulthood or an unhappy middle age do not necessarily tend to be unhappy in retirement also. Similarly, a thriving youth does not assure that one will be content after his working years have ended. Even big pensions are not that much important than people generally believe. For many people, retirement is the beginning of something entirely new.

In this research, it was also found that along with the factors of having a good sense of purpose and a happy marriage, learning how to be in action is an equally important feature of satisfied retirement. "Being in action" is referred to by scientists as participating in activities that are highly enjoyable, lack any monetary significance, must not cause any societal harm and do not automatically lead to public recognition and praise from others. After all the hard work of all these researchers, we can safely assume that happiness in retirement is based on a lot of different factors than those that promise a satisfied and economically contented middle age.

Social security and Pension

When you are in the middle of your working phase, you have to answer the question of: "Will you have enough income when you are retired to cover the living expenses?" Now besides other fruitful ways to earn stable income in the retiree years, there is always the attractive option of having social security. As you begin planning for retirement, you should keep in mind that you would also have social security providing you with a monthly income for life.

The amount of benefits you can get from social security is determined by three factors: The time period you have spent in the workforce, when you leave the workforce and how much money you have made during this time. The majority of the employees are covered by social security, with their employers automatically withholding social security taxes.

The common perception of social security is that it is merely a retirement program. Conversely, it also pays for survivors' and disability benefits as well. The Medicare hospital insurance is also funded by social security taxes. However, social security alone cannot provide sufficient amount for a secure retirement. That depends on how much you have been able to save up on your own and whether you are eligible for a pension from your company.

Social security provides vital financial support to millions of retirees. Because of its tremendous importance, you should know how its system works and what is the process which determines the amount of your benefits. Knowing all this will help make intelligent decisions when you have to leave and make sure that you will avoid making costly mistakes when you are planning your budget for retirement.

The retirement choices

The social security payments can be received at three different retirement levels:

At 62

You can retire early and take your social security payment at the age of 62 at the expense of reduction in monthly payments between 20% and 30%. The exact reduction percentage will depend upon your date of birth. By retiring early at 62, you will get spread the total amount receivable over a longer period of time which reduces each payment. Hence you will receive the same amount as you would have if you had retired at the normal retirement age, that is 65 plus.

Between 65 and 70

It is true that the normal or full retirement age is gradually moving up. Currently the averages show 67 to be the typical age people retire. But the standard is still 65 plus, however, the catch here is that you would exactly have to be "above" 65. This means that if you are turning 65 in 2015, you would have to wait a few months as you will not get full benefits until you are at least 10 months older than 65.

After 70

If you spend a few more years working and retire late, social security will give you a bonus to make up for the extra pay you contributed to the society. To put it in exact numbers, if you turned 65 in 2010 and you waited until now to retire, you will receive a 7.5% bonus for each year you have waited after the full retirement age. True, the number of payments will be less but the amount of each payment will be bigger.

Pension

Both private and public sector companies maintain and offer pension plans. When you are retired, you can collect both social security payments and a pension check monthly. There is an adverse effect of pension payments on social security benefits. However, a pension does not always reduce your social security, it depends upon the fact that whether your pension is from government or other non-covered work.

As discussed above, there are majorly two types of pension plans; private pension and public pension. Both have different criteria for payments and both have various different effects. We shall now see in detail how both of these help you in having a secure retirement.

Having A Private Pension Plan

These are offered by private companies. Usually private companies have different policies specific to each organization for pension plans but a general rule says that if you have worked in contracts that are covered by the company's social security policy, and you have paid social security taxes from each of your paycheck, then your pension plan will not have any sort of influence on your social security benefits.

Having a public pension plan

There are two regulations that affect your social security benefits if you have earned a public pension. Each is described below in detail.

Windfall Elimination Provision (WEP)

This provision is subject to public sector employees. If your employer did not entertain social security taxes from your salary and you have spent more than 10 years in jobs so that you are eligible for social security benefits, then you may be affected by WEP. This rule affects how disability or retirement benefits are provided and it may require a lesser social security plan.

It is limited to less than half of the aggregate of pension from the job that is not covered by social security. For instance, if your public sector pension is $500 a month, then WEP reduction will not be more than $250. It also affects the social security benefits of your dependent relatives. However, when you die, the WEP reduction will be removed and the dependent relatives will be returned to normal. At max, the WEP reduction can be $413.

Government Pension Offset (GPO)

It is subject to retirees receiving a pension from government jobs where they did not pay social security taxes. It offsets some or all of your spousal benefits. Generally, the spousal benefits in social security are equivalent to half the amount of worker's benefit if these benefits are claimed at the full retirement age and less than that if claimed earlier than 65 years of age. Similarly, the survivor benefits equals the full amount of employee's benefits if it is claimed at his full retirement age and less if it is requested at an earlier age.

The GPO shrinks the amount of retiree's social security benefits, both spousal and survivor, by 1/3 of your original pension amount. Let's say, you had received a monthly pension of $800, then two third of it: $530, is used to offset your spouse's or survivor benefit. If you qualified for a $500 spousal benefit, you would have $100 a month from social security accounts.

GPO comes with certain exemptions. Your social security benefits will not be reduced if you:

- Have a government pension plan that is not built on your own earnings.
- Are a local, state or federal government employee and your pension is based on a job in which you are bound to pay social security taxes.

Final say

The rules of WEP and GPO can be a bit complicated, but their impacts demand a careful review. To get more information on these rules, you can visit your social security office and if you want legal help, you should pay a visit to a nearby social security attorney.

Risk Balance

When you have a broad vision of achieving long-term goals, it means accepting that there will be a tradeoff between risk and return. To make informed decisions, you first need to understand the historical patterns that have occurred in the asset classes, to start off, you should at least know about the three primary asset classes.

Historically, stocks have provided investors with higher returns than cash or bonds but they have also always contained more risk. Bonds have offered less returns than stocks and more returns than cash, correspondingly, they have carried less risk than stocks but are riskier than cash. Cash is a relatively stable investment with much less risk than stocks or bonds but money in your pockets can not provide you with any return and further, there is also the probability of it failing to keep pace with inflation. Therefore, if you keep cash to avoid market risk, you may be exposed to a higher amount of purchasing power risk.

The task of balancing is all about how much you understand, accept and control risk. The majority of individuals try to balance risk by diversification of asset mix in their security portfolio. A retirement account with high diversity may consist of a combination of stocks, bonds and sometimes fixed-income funds like money market accounts. However, even in these three broad categories, there are further subdivisions of investments. For instance, a good portfolio may contain domestic and foreign stocks, or short term and long term bonds.

When you own a mix of such different types of securities in your retirement portfolio, it is quite possible to minimize the risk that comes along with any one specific type of investment. It has been observed that under the economic conditions that make stock prices decline, bonds perform better. Similarly, during the course of a bear market, money market accounts can deliver a more reliable income.

A very easy way to diverse your investments is to put money in mutual funds. They can provide access to hundreds of various securities in a single investment vehicle.

You could have a totally diversified portfolio which will incorporate several asset classes plus a broad range of security within each class as well simply by owning one diversified index fund. You can also try investing in securities that are from different sectors of the market; industries, countries, market capitalizations, etc.

When a person allocates his retirement funds to an asset class, whether he does so implicitly or explicitly, he should focus on controlling the risk factor. As the time passes, the risk factor becomes more and more volatile. Therefore, it is imperative that you should make sure that your retirement portfolio continues to maintain a balance between risk and return.

Inflation

How often did u use to hear your grandma talk about how she used to pay 20 cents to watch a movie? Or do you remember your own childhood? Do you remember how much a movie cost at that time? A whole lot less than it does now. That is the terrifying effect inflation has on our economies. No matter how much money you save for future, inflation can make its functionality much less than what its value is today. That is why the popular saying goes that

"Inflation Makes Retirement a Moving Target"

Erosion of savings.

Inflation does not actually decreases the amount of money you possess, what is does is that it reduces your purchasing power. If we assume that you are going to spend approximately the same amount in retirement as you are spending presently because you are going to engage in more leisure activities. Let us give an actual number to this value, let's say you are spending $40,000 a year.

Now to calculate how much money you would need to have a happy retirement, you need to know at what age you are planning to retire and how long will you really live after retirement. Oh, that is a complex question but here we have world bank's surveys to estimate an answer, according to it the average life expectancy was 78 years in 2010. Hence, if we assume that you are going to leave the workforce at the age of 65, you have to provide for 13 more years of retirement. If we are to assume that you are going to spend $40,000 a year in your retirement then you would need to amass (13 x $4000) or $520000 for your retiree years.

The issue here is that $40,000 in the year 2020 would be able to purchase fewer goods or services than it could in 2015 and in 2025, $40,000 will probably have even less purchasing power than it could in 2020. Get the whole picture? You cannot plan to use the exact equal amount of dollars year after year and assume that your needs will be fulfilled exactly the same way. So in retirement, you have to give certain adjustment to your budget after every few years to make up for the cost of living. Only this way you can continue to purchase goods and supplies the same way as you do now.

The concern with inflation lifts off when you think about its relationship with the interest rates of economy. However, being carefree due to this regard does not do well for a happy retirement. If you have a savings account (which you should have if you are a careful person), the interest rate it pays is likely to be a lot less than the rate of inflation. This means that the prices of goods and services are climbing up much faster than the value of money in your account.

Depletion of budgets

You need to remind yourself that once in retirement you will not be a full-time wage payee therefore the importance of budgeting for that period is quite tremendous. To ensure that your savings will last throughout your retirement period, you will need to establish an intelligent budget. Inflation has a diminishing effect on budgets. For all the reasons stated earlier, you need to account for inflation in your budget planning.

Some core concerns

Happiness comes secondary to the fulfillment of basic needs in all psychological studies. Therefore, before you can begin comprehending how inflation can affect your hobbies and other activities, you need to be especially cognizant of its effect in a few areas of basic needs:

Food costs

What is the most basic need of staying alive? Yes, you guessed from the heading; food. Food prices are commonly observed to be very volatile. You can never be sure what to expect when it comes to something whose production depends very highly on the environmental conditions. Take beef, grains or dairy prices, for example, recently their prices have spiked due to the unanticipated factors such as drought, livestock illness and even change in farming practices.

There is no saying what will happen 20 years later to some farm that is responsible for producing the food you need on your table. Expect the same kind of uncertainty in the future. As no one can put a number on the amount of uncertainty, I can tell you that you should just keep as wide a cushion as possible for such discrepancies and the rest will go fine.

Medical costs

Think about the primary reason for retirement: You are retired because you cannot keep up with the amount of work that you can do when you are young. This means that in retirement, you will most probably need more medical care than you do at a working age. A concern develops here that the medical costs are always on the rise. In addition to that their pace is significantly greater than the current CPI inflation averages. Therefore when you are budgeting, you need to take specific care to account for medical inflation as things can go seriously wrong if something goes awry.

Fuel costs

Why is fuel price important? Fuel is the source which provides you what you need at your doorstep. The cost of food that you have on your table, the medicine that you need to sooth your back pain or even the newspaper that you read every day includes in it the cost of fuel that took to transport it. Therefore, the price of most goods is likely to increase if the fuel prices rise. Besides this shipping cost, if you are preparing to travel in your retirement, change in fuel costs can have a tremendous impact on your costs of driving or flying. These prices are also very uncertain and have a lot of unpredictable variables like geopolitics, environmental changes, etc. Therefore again, for this you also need to have the widest cushion of risk-protection as possible.

How to Keep Things Going During Retirement

Retirement is an act of maintaining a perfect balance between saving and expenditure. You would want to use enough money to enjoy your life to the fullest while taking care that you can take care of your future needs as well. If you can preserve this balance, then there is little reason to worry about running out of money.

Here we ask the question; what are the factors that throw people off balance even after they have planned a very efficient budget? The primary reason for this is that as much meticulous they are about their retirement savings at a young age, they become just as much thoughtless in retirement about the little things that hold great significance. Here we shall talk about several measures you can take to avoid ending up with a nasty surprise from your bank manager.

Have a measuring device

What would happen if you are driving across the state without a fuel tank gauge? How will you when you have to stop for gas? I think you would need to take a guess for that and a guess doesn't always give you the correct answer. So there is a huge chance that you might end up in the middle of the road with no fuel in your car.

Similarly, if your approach to retirement savings is same, you might end up getting yourself into trouble even when you have planned a healthy budget. Once you are retired, it doesn't mean that you can start getting lax about using up your savings. You should put a monitoring process and make a habit of checking up on your retirement account after every big expense.

You can measure the income coming from your investments and take its ratio with your expenditures, habitually check upon how much liquid money you have left and make adjustments according to it. With luck, this monitoring process can also tell you that you can afford to spend more just like the gas gauge doesn't always tell the driver when to slow down, but also when to accelerate.

Have a plan B

Life is full of unexpected mishaps and it is not just limited to the working age when you are thinking about so many things, this will continue when you are retired. If you using up all the assets you had in your budget plan, you would have a great risk of losing all your money. You will have to allocate some asset amount to a reserve account, which you would have to promise yourself that you will only use in emergencies. You will not include this set of assets in your spending plan for living expenses.

It is not necessary that your reserves are liquid: they can be home equity, a piece of land or maybe even a valuable collector's item. With luck, you will never need to use up this reserve, but just in case you do need money for emergencies, you will have an ample amount to deal with life's discrepancies. No one can tell you when life is going to throw you off track, the best you can do is to be ready for it.

Be aware of scammers

The world is full of people who will try their best to separate you from your beloved money. Even in families, there are those relatives that can mooch out money from you in the name of caregiving. Many a times it has been observed that a lot of retirees fall for scams that assure them extraordinary returns. Yes, this is a bitter fact that as you age, your cognitive ability to weigh between financial choices decline. In contrast to that, many retirees believe that they can still perform as well financially as they used to in their prime. This becomes a very dangerous combination.

You need a reliable advisor for monetary matters, whether it is a family member or some other professional. You should consult them before making any significant financial decision. Especially when someone is pressuring you with an offer, you can evade this pressure by telling them that you need to consult your advisor for this.

Insurance

As we have informed you about how much your health and other such costs will change, it will affect your insurance needs too. A majority of the retirees dump disability insurance coverage as this policy is structured to replace your salary if you become unable to work due to any disability. It is not worth a cost after retirement.

You can also let go of life insurance coverage when you retire. The basic purpose of it is to support your family if you die suddenly. But when you have saved so assiduously and do not have anyone who is dependent on you, this coverage's expenses will become redundant. However, you should consult your financial advisor before canceling your coverage.

Core things to consider when working out the retirement budget

Being happy is important, obviously, but you cannot be happy when you are lying sick in bed and you don't have enough money to pay up for medical emergencies as you have spent your entire savings in achieving contentment in retirement.

There are some things which are the basic necessity of life. Without them, you cannot survive. These are the elementary prerequisites of spending a good life. From the beginning of your career, when you first took financial responsibility, they start show their impacts and force you to assign a healthy amount of money to take care of them.

When in working age, you can create a cash flow easily enough to maintain their sustenance but when you retire, you lose the control you had earlier on the situation. Therefore when you are planning your budget, you need to keep in mind these factors and assign them a cautious amount so that you can have a comfortable retirement.

Housing

Think back, what was the first thing you had to do when you got out of your parent's house and the hostel they paid for? You looked for a house of your own. Having a roof over your head is one of the most basic needs, indicated by psychologists, financial gurus and other academic scholars everywhere. A house is a symbol of belonging to people. It performs as their root to nature, somewhere where they can come to relax when they are tired of the world outside. Getting out, travelling to luscious places of the world, nothing means as much if you do not have a house.

When you are retired, you would not a healthy income source therefore the payment of mortgages becomes crucial as when you retire you would at least need to have a house of your own that is not being held as security in a bank. You need to own a house in when you are retired. So make sure that you pay your mortgages before you retire, or as soon as possible.

Also, when retired, some people prefer to live in a healthy environment or have a house with beautiful scenery. If you have such plans, you need to make specific adjustments to your budget plan. Having a house at such a place can lead to health benefits as well.

Food

Food is the most basic thing you need to spend money for in retirement. How many times do you need food a day? What budget you need to provide for in your daily routine. To have a general view of this concept, you can assume that you would need the same amount and type of food when you retire. Now think about the average age of death in the US and multiply your current yearly budget for food with the number of years after retirement. This way, you can get an approximate estimate of the money you are going to need in retirement for diet.

You should also keep in mind the factor of inflation. The prices of food items change regularly and with too much uncertainty to formulate a pattern. It is highly probable that the prices of food items after 5 or 10 years will be much more than they are now. You would need to provide sufficient amount of money that you are able to cope with at least the mild price changes.

Clothing

When you are planning a big budget for a huge number of years, the small things are bound to get ignored. But they have their significant nonetheless. Fortunately for you, clothing is an expense that reduces drastically when you finish your career. But you would still need to plan for a small budget that you can put aside especially for clothing. Your clothes show your inner personality. You would not want to lose your flair when you are retired. You would still need to dress smartly and if you are planning to go to international tours, you would need to dress accordingly and therefore you will need to plan accordingly as well.

Household goods and services

Household goods are always breaking and always demanding a repair or in the worst case scenario, replacement. This is also a cost that reduces when you are retired, but nonetheless you would need to have a stable amount to make do with these costs.

Similarly, there are household services that you always require to make sure you have a healthy, fitting and pleasant living environment. Once retired, the importance of these services increase. The costs would more or less remain same but they will become more significant as you would be spending more time at home and the more pleasant it is, the better its effect will be on your happiness and health.

Health

It is a natural phenomenon that health deteriorates with each passing age. When you are young, you are at the pinnacle of health. Once you grow old, more diseases will hit you and you will be more likely to get sick. Hence, your doctor's payment will increase by a huge amount.

The best option in working age is to keep aside some money for health emergencies, when you are retired you will not be able to buff up that account, therefore you need to provide for that when you are saving up for retirement. Similar to the case of prices of food items, the factor of economic fluctuations becomes important here as well as the prices of medicines and medical services are likely to increase due to inflation. Thus here also, you need to have a safe strategy to keep a cushion of protection in case of price increase.

Further reading

A Beginner's Investing Guide Learn The Strategies To Smart Investing And Start Making Real Money

This book will be of value to both beginner investors who need a strong, yet clear grasp of the investing concepts, as well as seasoned investors looking to add some applicable knowledge to their investing portfolio.

As with any other skill, you can learn how to invest. It all comes down to understanding the concepts that are at play, taking smart action today and fine-tuning your approach in time.

You will finish reading the book with a fundamental understanding of what is out there and how you will fit in the investing world.
It will be like going on a walk with a knowledgeable friend who really wants to help you succeed.

Options Trading: Best Investing Strategies For Beginners to Make Money By Knowing The Simple Basics

Options Trading is the next greatest thing in the investment area that promises huge wealth.

My book will provide you with clear, concise information that's easy to apply. By the time you're done, you'll have a fundamental knowledge of investing using Options Trading, and be equipped with all the information you need to make forward bounds in this field. It will be like going on a walk with a knowledgeable friend who really wants to help you succeed.

How to Retire Happy, Wild, and Free

How to Retire Happy, Wild, and Free provides readers encouraging advice on how they can enjoy life to its fullest. The book shows how the key to a gratified retirement encompasses over leisure activities, physical and mental well-being, creative pursuits and concrete social support. This book provides a holistic approach to the fears, dreams, and expectations that people possess about retirement.

It goes beyond plain numbers, which is usually the primary focus of most of the retirement authors. The wisdom that the writer offers is much more important than the amount of money you have saved. He creates a happy, active and satisfied retirement in a way that does not require millions of dollars.

The 5 Years Before You Retire: Retirement Planning When You Need It the Most

This book provides a complete guide for planning the retirement budget. It trains you to plan a budget when you think it is too late to start saving up. This book explains step by step what to do in the remaining five years to get maximum profit from your current investments and help you to formulate a practical retirement plan.

It takes you through each of the crucial financial, familial and medical choices you can think about and covers every aspect of retirement planning. It provides straightforward strategies and explains each in detail so that you can make the most of the last few years of your working life and provide for the future that you always envisioned.

How to Retire the Cheapskate Way

Yeager serves as an official Savings Expert for AARP. In this book he takes a differing approach to other writers in retirement planning and focuses on making a compelling case that every retiree can have a fun, anxiety-free retirement lifestyle simply by spending smartly and focusing on his goals and realistic expectations from retirement.

This book combines the power of humor with quirky anecdotes that have made Yeager a much-loved writer. *How to Retire the Cheapskate Way* provides the readers with countless retirement tips and secrets including how to size up your lifestyle for a better retirement.

Get What's Yours: The Secrets to Maxing Out Your Social Security

Social security is a huge and confusing maze which is impossible to navigate without expert help. This is a great book if you want to know more about social security. This book shows exactly how you can maximize your social security benefits and increase your earnings.

It shows how you can enter this perplexing maze and surface with maximum benefits in your hands. The writers explain the gist of 2,728 rules of social security process in a comprehensible and user-friendly manner. It covers the most common scenarios met by retired married couples, divorced retirees and widows, and widowers. It elucidates what you can do it you are retired and you have the responsibility for children or disabled beneficiary. It explains how to plan well before retirement.

Furthermore, it talks about the tax component in budget planning and its impact on your choices along with the financial implications for if you decide to pursue other investment options. It is probably the best book to elaborate on social security so clearly and offers a conversational and thorough analysis of different situations retirees have to face.

Your Free Gift

I wanted to show my appreciation that you support my work so I've put together a free gift for you.

"Retirement Cheat Sheet"

Just visit the link below to download it now:

http://pozittron.wix.com/musthavepublishing#!gift/c17z6

I know you will love this gift.

If you have 30 seconds,
Leave a Quick Review!

Thanks!
Scott Thomas

Disclaimer and Terms of Use: Effort has been made to ensure that the information in this book is accurate and complete, however, the author and the publisher do not warrant the accuracy of the information, text and graphics contained within the book due to the rapidly changing nature of science, research, known and unknown facts and internet. The Author and the publisher do not hold any responsibility for errors, omissions or contrary interpretation of the subject matter herein. This book is presented solely for motivational and informational purposes only.

www.ingramcontent.com/pod-product-compliance
Lightning Source LLC
Chambersburg PA
CBHW071007180526
45168CB00003B/1321